Wild World

Watching
Dolphins
in the Oceans

Elizabeth Miles

Heinemann Library
Chicago, Illinois

Customer Service 888-454-2279

Visit our website at www.heinemannraintree.com

Designed by Ron Kamen and edesign
Illustrations by Martin Sanders
Printed and bound in China by South China Printing Company

10 09 08 07 06
10 9 8 7 6 5 4 3 2 1

Library of Congress Cataloging-in-Publication Data

Miles, Elizabeth, 1960-
  Watching dolphins in the ocean / Elizabeth Miles.
    p. cm. -- (Wild world)
  Includes bibliographical references and index. ISBN 1-4034-7229-7 (library binding - hardcover) --
ISBN 1-4034-7242-4 (pbk.) I. Dolphins--Juvenile literature. I. Title. II. Series: Wild world (Chicago, Ill.)
QL737.C432M53 2006
599.53'09162--dc22

                    2005016781

Acknowledgments

The author and publishers are grateful to the following for permission to reproduce copyright material: Alamy pp. **7**
(Stephen Frink Collection), **29** (Stephen Frink Collection); Ardea pp. **4** (Augusto Stanzani), **21** (Tom and Pat Leeson), **22**,
23 (Augusto Stanzani), **28** (Ralf Kiefner); Bruce Coleman p. **19** (Jorg & Petra Wegner); Corbis p. **27** (Guigo Constant);
FLPA pp. **12** (Tui de Roy), **20** (Michael Gore); Getty Images pp. **8**, **9**; Nature PL pp. **18** (Doug Perrine), **26** (Jeff Rotman);
PhotoLibrary.com pp. **5** (IFA-Bilderteam Gmbh), **10** (Gerard Soury), **11** (David Fleetham), **13** (Daniel Cox), **14** (IFA-
Bilderteam Gmbh), **15** (Norbert Wu), **16** (Pacific Stock), **24** (Konrad Wothe), **25** (Konrad Wothe); Zefa p. **17** (Masterfile).

Cover photographs of dolphins reproduced with permission of Seapics/Ingrid Visser.

The publishers would like to thank Michael Bright for his assistance in the preparation of this book. Every effort has been
made to contact copyright holders of any material reproduced in this book. Any omissions will be rectified in subsequent
printings if notice is given to the publishers. The paper used to print this book comes from sustainable resources.

Some words are shown in bold, **like this**. You can find out
what they mean by looking in the glossary.

Contents

Meet the Dolphins

This is the ocean, the home of bottlenose dolphins. Dolphins live in oceans, rivers, and lakes around the world. They are not fish. They are **mammals**, like us.

▶▶ *Dolphins spend most of their time swimming under water.*

There are 32 kinds of dolphin that live in the ocean. We are going to watch bottlenose dolphins. You often see these in marine parks, but most live in the wild.

▲ *Although they are called whales, killer whales are part of the dolphin family.*

Underwater Homes

Bottlenose dolphins live in oceans in many parts of the world. Many of them live off the east **coast** of North America. The water is not too cold there.

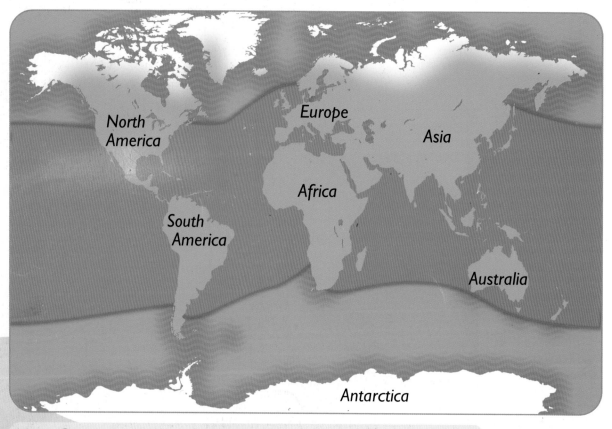

North America

Europe

Asia

Africa

South America

Australia

Antarctica

Key ● This color shows where dolphins live in the oceans.

▲ *Bottlenose dolphins are friendly and do not mind if people are close by.*

Many bottlenose dolphins stay close to the coast. They can catch plenty of fish here, without diving too deep. They often swim in bays or **harbors**.

There's a Dolphin!

Spotting a bottlenose is very exciting. Its skin looks smooth and rubbery. Under the skin, there is a layer of fat called blubber. It keeps the dolphin warm.

▶▶ *The bottlenose got its name because people think its nose, or snout, is shaped like a bottle.*

▼ *A bottlenose's smooth-shaped body helps it glide through the water.*

Bottlenoses are dark gray. They have a light gray patch on their belly. Their color matches the dark ocean water. This helps them to hide from **predators**.

Blowholes

Dolphins cannot breathe under water like fish can. Dolphins have **lungs**, like people do. They have to come up for air.

▼ *Dolphins come up to breathe every two to four minutes.*

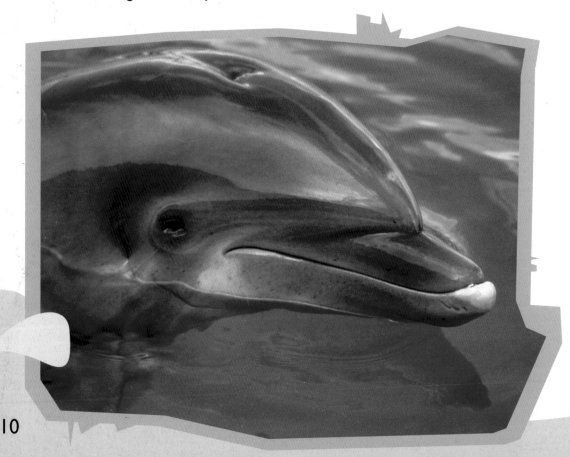

A dolphin breathes through a blowhole on the top of its head. It closes the blowhole when it dives under water. Water cannot get in when the blowhole is closed.

blowhole

⯅ *A dolphin's blowhole is like a **nostril**.*

Swimming in the Ocean

Dolphins swim by flapping their tail and **flukes** up and down. Their smooth body moves quickly through the water. They use their **flippers** to turn and to stop.

▼ *The **fin** on the bottlenose's back stops the dolphin from rolling around in the water.*

flipper

fin

flukes

Bottlenoses are very good at jumping. Sometimes they jump for fun. When they land, the splash lets other dolphins know where they are.

▲ *Bottlenoses can take a breath of air*
when they jump.

Ocean Food

Bottlenoses eat fish and squid. They grab their **prey** with their teeth. They do not chew their food. Instead, they swallow it whole.

▼ *Dolphins learn to eat fish that is good for them, such as mullet.*

To find fish to eat, dolphins make clicking noises. The sound of the clicks bounces off the fish as an **echo**. This tells dolphins where the fish are.

▲ *The echo tells the dolphins if there is anything there, such as a **shoal** of fish to eat.*

Migration

In summer, the bottlenoses swim north. There are more fish to eat there. The dolphins swim for days to reach new places to feed.

▼ *People in boats sometimes follow dolphins on their journey.*

▲ *When bottlenose dolphins migrate, they travel in large groups, called herds, of up to 100.*

In winter, there are fewer fish to eat. The bottlenoses swim south again. They **migrate** north and south every year.

Living Together

Dolphins usually live in small groups called pods. There are about seven dolphins in a pod. If one dolphin is sick, the others will help it stay afloat.

▼ *A pod of dolphins hunts together. These dolphins are rounding up a **shoal** of fish to eat.*

⬆ *Groups of dolphins like to swim and jump together.*

Dolphins make whistling and clicking noises to **communicate** with each other. They also send messages by slapping their **flukes** on the surface of the water.

Finding a Mate

In fall it is time for **male** dolphins to find **females** to **mate** with. They may have to fight for a female. Female dolphins are called cows.

▼ *Male dolphins are called bulls. These bulls are fighting over a female.*

The male that wins the fight goes to the female. Before mating, the male and female might swim together. They may touch **flippers** or even **butt** heads.

▼ *It is hard to see which is the bull and which is the cow.*

Babies

In fall, one year after she has mated, the **female** bottlenose gives birth. A baby dolphin is called a calf. Calves are paler than adults.

▼ *Calves are born tail first. They swim to the surface to take their first breath of air.*

▲ *Mother dolphins stay close to their calves.*

The mother can produce milk. She feeds
milk to her calf for more than a year. She
will look after the calf for many years.

Young Calves

The calf soon learns to swim around. It learns to recognize the sound of its mother's whistle. When the mother whistles, the calf will come to her side.

▼ *A young calf often swims beside its mother.* **Predators** *cannot easily see it there.*

Groups of **females** often live together.
They help look after each other's calves.
One mother goes off to hunt, while the
others babysit her calf.

▲ *In a few years, these calves will be old*
enough to leave their mothers.

Dolphins in Danger

The calves learn to protect themselves from sharks and **orcas**. Dolphins use their head as a battering ram to fight off these **predators**.

▶▶ *Sharks sometimes hide and wait for dolphins to swim by.*

A diver will help this dolphin get free. Many others die in nets like these.

Some people kill dolphins for food. Lots of dolphins get stuck in fishing nets. If a calf survives these dangers, it should live to be about 30 years old.

Tracker's Guide

When you want to watch animals in the wild, you need to find them first. Dolphins can be hard to find because they live in the oceans.

▲ *You must look carefully to spot a dolphin. They often swim at the front of big boats.*

⬆ Some people go on dolphin-watching trips. Bottlenose dolphins are well known for being friendly with people.

Glossary

butt hit something with your head

coast land area next to the ocean

communicate pass on information. Talking is a way of communicating.

echo sound that bounces back so you hear it again

female animal that can become a mother when it is grown up. Girls and women are female people.

fin part that sticks out from the top of a fish, dolphin, or whale

flipper fin that sticks out from the side of a dolphin like an arm

flukes two parts that make up a dolphin's tail

harbor sheltered part of the coast, where boats are often kept

lungs parts inside the body that you use to breathe air in and out

male animal that can become a father when it is grown up. Boys and men are male people.

mammal group of animals that feed their babies their own milk and have some hair on their bodies

mate when male and female animals produce young

migrate travel a long distance, following the same journey every year

nostril hole that you breathe through. Your nose has two nostrils.

orca another name for a killer whale

predator animal that catches and eats other animals for food

prey animal that gets caught and eaten by other animals

shoal group of fish

Find Out More

Books

Arnold, Nick. *Diving with Dolphins*. New York: Scholastic, 2004.

Carwardine, Mark. *Whales, Dolphins, and Porpoises*. New York: Dorling Kindersley, 2002.

Eckart, Edana. *Bottlenose Dolphins*. New York: Children's Press, 2003.

Gentle, Victor, and Janet Perry. *Bottlenose Dolphins*. Milwaukee: Gareth Stevens, 2001.

Laskey, Elizabeth. *Sea Creatures: Dolphins*. Chicago: Heinemann Library, 2003.

Lynch, Emma. *Ocean Food Chains*. Chicago: Heinemann Library, 2004.

Miles, Elizabeth. *Why Do Animals Have Wings, Fins and Flippers?* Chicago: Heinemann Library, 2002.

Murray, Julie. *Bottle-Nosed Dolphins*. Edina, Minn.: ABDO, 2004.

Pyers, Greg. *Ocean Explorer*. Chicago: Raintree, 2004.

Index